All About Animals
Meerkats

By Justine Ciovacco

Reader's Digest Young Families

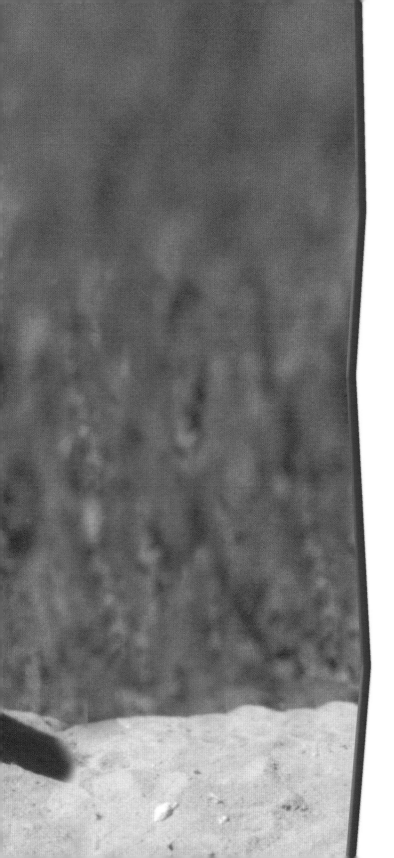

Contents

Chapter 1
A Meerkat's Day

Another Name
Some people call a meerkat a suricate (pronounced *SUHR ih cate*). That's because the meerkat's scientific name is *suricata suricatta*.

A small group of meerkats wander through a dry grassy area of South Africa's Kalahari Desert. They stay close together for safety. And they don't travel too far away from their burrow. They want to be able to watch over a special entrance hole today. Inside the burrow, Mama Meerkat is getting ready to give birth. Papa Meerkat runs down inside to check on her and then back outside to look for food with the group. He's been through this with Mama a few times before.

In a little while, Mama gives birth to three kits. Their eyes and ears are closed. Their bodies have only a few patches of fur. Immediately Mama licks them clean. She then nudges their little bodies around to help them figure out how to drink her milk.

Wild Words

Meerkats live together in a group called a **mob** *or a* **colony**. *The meerkats that have the most young are called the* **alpha female** *and the* **alpha male**. *All meerkat babies are called* **kits**.

After ten days, the kits' ears and eyes open. When the kits are about four weeks old, they stop drinking milk. The adult members of the colony bring bits of food to them. At about the same time, the kits are allowed to take short trips outside the burrow. They are growing up fast! The adults watch over them and take them for walks.

The kits are fully grown when they are six months old. Now they can freely move around outside the burrows, soak up the sun, and play. But they also must learn to hunt for food.

The kits are taught to hunt by a female member of the group. But she is not their mother. Her special job is teaching—she teaches all the young kits born into the group how to hunt. She is great at tracking the scent of insects under the sand. Plus, she's an expert at catching and cutting up a scorpion!

First, the kits watch their teacher as she runs her snout along the sand in search of insects. She hears something moving below the surface, and so she begins digging down through the sand with her sharp claws. As soon as she sees the insect, she quickly jabs at it and gobbles it down.

The kits begin to follow her lead and look for their own places to dig. The older meerkats will continue to bring them food until the youngsters are able to find food completely on their own.

Family First

A meerkat is ready to be a mother or father when it is a year old. But it may have to wait until its own mom and dad stop having youngsters. Until then, the young adults know that they must help take care of their new brothers and sisters.

Safety in Numbers

Meerkats know they have no time to waste when they gather together to scare away a predator. Some predators see a mob of meerkats as one large animal instead of a lot of small ones, and they decide to turn away.

One morning, just as the sun rises, all the meerkats pop up out of their burrow as they always do. After lying in the sun for a while, they begin to look for food. One meerkat stands on guard and watches for predators. He sees an eagle flying above the colony's territory. At once, he starts making a high-pitched peeping sound to warn the group to get ready for a fight.

A few adults rush the kits back into the burrow. The remaining adults gather together. They quickly start digging in the sand to create big puffs of dust. This confuses the eagle and makes the meerkats hard to see. At the same time, the meerkats all stand up on their hind legs. They begin to stretch their bodies up straight, and they move closer together. Next, growling and snarling, they start jumping up and down. They are trying to look like one giant, scary animal. And it works! The lone eagle turns and flies away.

Together, the meerkats have saved their lives! Pretty soon it will be time to return to their burrow for another night of cuddling and sleeping.

Wild Warrior

If a meerkat can't get to its burrow when an attack is near, it may decide to lie down on its back. But it's not playing dead. It waves its claws around wildly and opens its mouth to show its teeth. This meerkat is showing the predator that it has many sharp tools ready!

Chapter 2
The Meerkat's Body

A meerkat's tail is like a bike's kickstand—it helps the meerkat stand up straight on its hind legs without losing its balance.

Body Basics

All meerkats have a coat that is a mix of gray, orange, and tan fur—except for the throat, which is a grayish white color. Dark-brown stripes run across their backs. Each meerkat has its own unique stripe pattern!

All meerkats have a tail with a black tip. The tail is usually the same color as the meerkat's stripes. The black tip is a big help to meerkats. They keep their tails up in the air when they look for food so they can easily spot one another! The tail can be as long as 8 inches.

Meerkats need to rest often because they use a lot of energy watching for danger and searching for food. This is one reason meerkats spend a lot of time basking in the sun. Meerkats can even stretch out in the noonday sun because their bodies do not overheat.

Hot Spot

A meerkat's belly has a small patch with almost no hair on it. A meerkat's dark skin shows through underneath. This patch helps a meerkat regulate its body temperatrue.

Face Facts

A meerkat's face makes a real point! Its nose sticks out two to three inches from its face. Inside its snout are tiny, sharp teeth. Meerkats have four long canine teeth that help them tear meat. Their twelve back teeth help them slice food for easy swallowing.

Meerkats spend a lot of time in the sand, and most of that time is spent digging. Their eyes and ears help them deal with every sandy day. The meerkat's eyelid has a special membrane. It acts like a windshield wiper by removing sand from the eye with each blink. Meerkats can see faraway things very well and at angles around them.

The tiny half-moon shaped ears of meerkats stick out from the sides of their heads. But, amazingly, the ears don't fill up with dirt while the meerkats are digging. This is because meerkats can close their ears to make the openings very small.

Surely Sharp

The meerkat's four sharp canine teeth are typical of animals that eat only meat. Canine teeth hold onto prey so it can't run away.

The dark circles around a meerkat's eyes make the eyes appear larger to some animals. This may even help scare them away! The dark circles also absorb some of the sun's rays, which lets meerkats look directly at the sun while watching out for a swooping eagle.

Meerkats are very fast diggers. They can dig out as much dirt as their own body weight in a couple of seconds!

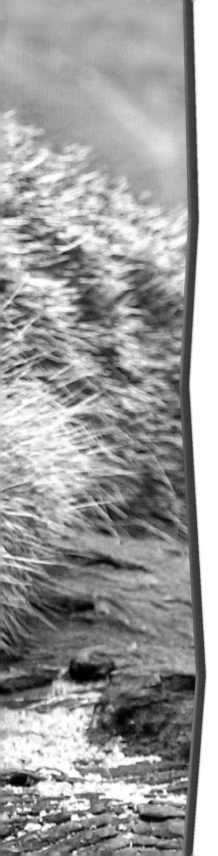

Dig Those Claws

Meerkats use all four paws when they dig, which helps them to dig very quickly. Each paw has four sharp claws that are about a half-inch long. The claws stick out all the time and are curved, making them great for digging.

Meerkats also use their sharp claws to kill prey swiftly. Sometimes they will then drag the prey, such as a millipede, across the sand with the tips of their claws. To meerkats and some other animals, millipedes have an awful smell and taste. Dragging a millipede through the sand seems to help "clean" it and make it more appealing to eat.

Meerkats are excellent climbers. They climb with great ease, much like cats. Their claws are a big help, as are their strong back legs.

Tippy Toes

A meerkat looks very tall when it stands on its back legs. The paws on the back legs are long. Meerkats do not stand on the soles of their feet, as people do. They stand on their toes.

Chapter 3
The Mob Rules

Baby-sitters may go without food for as long as a day while they watch over the colony's newborns.

All for One

Meerkats live in groups of three to five families. These groups, which may total up to 40 members, are called mobs or colonies. Each meerkat in a mob usually has its own job, but it will also share jobs with other meerkats when needed. The most important point about mob-living is that all the members help each other when looking for food, teaching and protecting their young, and defending against predators.

All meerkat jobs are very special. Here's what they do:

• Hunters look for food. All meerkats do this for themselves most of the time, but hunters help find food for the kits. They will also find food for the baby-sitters.

• Baby-sitters stay near the den with the kits and protect them while the other meerkats are hunting. Female baby-sitters provide milk for the young, just like their moms.

• Teachers show young meerkats how to hunt for food.

• Guards, also known as sentinels, watch the land and sky for predators. They usually stand up on their hind legs on top of a high spot, such as a log or a mound of sand. They sound out warning signals if they see, hear, or smell a predator.

A is for Alpha

Meerkat mobs do not have one meerkat as the leader. However, there is an alpha male and an alpha female that usually have all or almost all of the babies. They sometimes act as the leaders because their jobs are so important. If other meerkats have children, they risk being kicked out of the mob by the alphas.

Most alpha females give birth about once a year. One female can have as many as thirty-two kits in her lifetime. Alphas need a lot of help with all of the kits they have!

A meerkat usually stays with the family it was born into and with the colony in which it grew up. If the colony gets too large because of many new births, a meerkat that is ready to mate may move into another colony.

Single females are usually welcomed into other colonies. Males have a harder time if the new colony already has a strong alpha male who is not ready to give up his job. If the group has a big enough territory, a large colony might divide into two separate ones.

Move On!

When a meerkat colony has eaten all the available food in one area, they move on and dig new burrows in another area. Most colonies move four or five times a year.

Staying close together and grooming each other helps the members of a meerkat mob to work as a group.

Meerkats usually hide and run from each other before settling down to wrestling, their favorite kind of play-fighting.

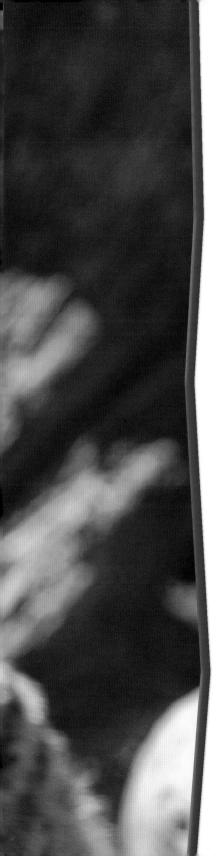

Fighting for Their Rights

Meerkats enjoy wrestling and fighting with each other. It's a game, but it's also a way for them to show their feelings. Young kits will wrestle over food that adults have brought to them. Adults don't mind this kind of play-fighting because it helps the young ones practice defending themselves against predators.

Females also make fighting moves, such as jumping and snapping, to let males know they are ready to mate.

Cool and Careful

Meerkats are very smart and learn fast. They are one of the few animals that are actually "taught" how to hunt for food by their elders.

Meerkats are said to have short memories. Why? Because they have been known to kill any meerkat that has been away from the colony for more than six hours! The meerkats in the colony are often just being extra careful, in case the lone meerkat turns out to be an attacker. If the meerkats are able to stay calm and take the time to smell the new arrival, they can figure out that they already know him.

Home Sweet Home

Meerkat mobs live together in underground homes called burrows. The burrows, which are dug by the meerkats, are made up of long tunnels that connect separate rooms. The average meerkat burrow is about 10 feet long and has about 15 rooms. Each burrow can have up to 70 entrances so the meerkats can quickly run inside to hide! These entrances are all connected by tunnels.

Inside the burrow, a meerkat mob is protected from the sun's extreme heat and the nighttime's extreme cold. On cold nights, the members of the colony gather in groups and huddle together underground to stay warm.

Meerkats mark the entrances to their burrow with saliva and urine to warn other animals away. They move into a newly made burrow about every other month, depending on the supply of food. They will always stay in the burrow where their young were born for about three weeks. They will not move until the kits are strong enough to do so.

Sometimes meerkats will share their home with ground squirrels and yellow mongooses. These three types of animals don't eat the same foods, so they can share a territory. However, meerkats keep their newborns safe by keeping them away from the visitors.

Meerkats leave their burrow entrances one at a time. This way, the first one out can look for danger.

Chapter 4
The Meerkat Menu

Meerkats spend up to four or five hours a day searching for food. While digging in the sand for a meal, they sometimes dig themselves into a hole — and entirely out of sight — without even realizing it!

Fast Food

Meerkats are carnivores (pronounced *CAR nih vorz*), which means they only eat meat. They are swift hunters that can grab small, fast-moving food such as worms, millipedes, crickets, beetles, and other insects. They are also able to catch and eat small mammals, lizards, and some snakes.

Meerkats are one of the few animals in the world that kill and eat scorpions. Although scorpions have deadly poison on their stingers, adult meerkats are able to bite off the stingers and survive.

It takes a lot of practice for meerkat kits to learn to kill scorpions. At first, adult meerkats catch and kill the tasty meal for the kits. They even bite off the poisonous stingers before giving them to the little ones. As the days go by, the lessons get tougher. The adults bite the stingers off live scorpions, but the kits must kill the now harmless creatures by themselves. The adults will even bring a scorpion back if it runs away from the kit's tiny claws. After a lot of practice, all meerkat kits are able to hunt and kill scorpions by the time they are four months old.

On the Lookout

Meerkats find a lot of their food by looking and listening downward. Keeping their heads down makes them easy targets for predators, such as jackals, hyenas, snakes, eagles, and even members of other meerkat mobs that move into their territory.

So some meerkats stand guard while the other meerkats hunt for food. The guards make a low, steady peeping sound when all is well. But they will change to a fast, high-pitched peeping sound as a warning the minute one of them sees a predator.

The meerkat's excellent vision makes it possible for it to spot an animal more than one thousand feet away—that's farther than three football fields!

Meerkats act quickly when they know a predator is near. First, they try to dive underground or under any thorny bushes. If there is nowhere to hide, they will come together and fluff out their fur. They will jump up and down. They'll even hiss and snarl in the hopes of scaring the predator away. Baby-sitters don't join in these group scare demonstrations. Their job is to find a place to hide the kits. If they can't find a hole, they may lie on top of the young ones to keep them safe!

Human Interest

Meerkats quickly learn which animals are dangerous and which can be ignored. Scientists found that over time meerkats learn to ignore people watching and photographing them. They will even move closer to see what the humans are doing.

A guard, or sentinel, will stand in place and watch for enemies for an hour or two at a time. Then a new guard will take over.

Chapter 5
Meerkats in the World

Where Meerkats Live

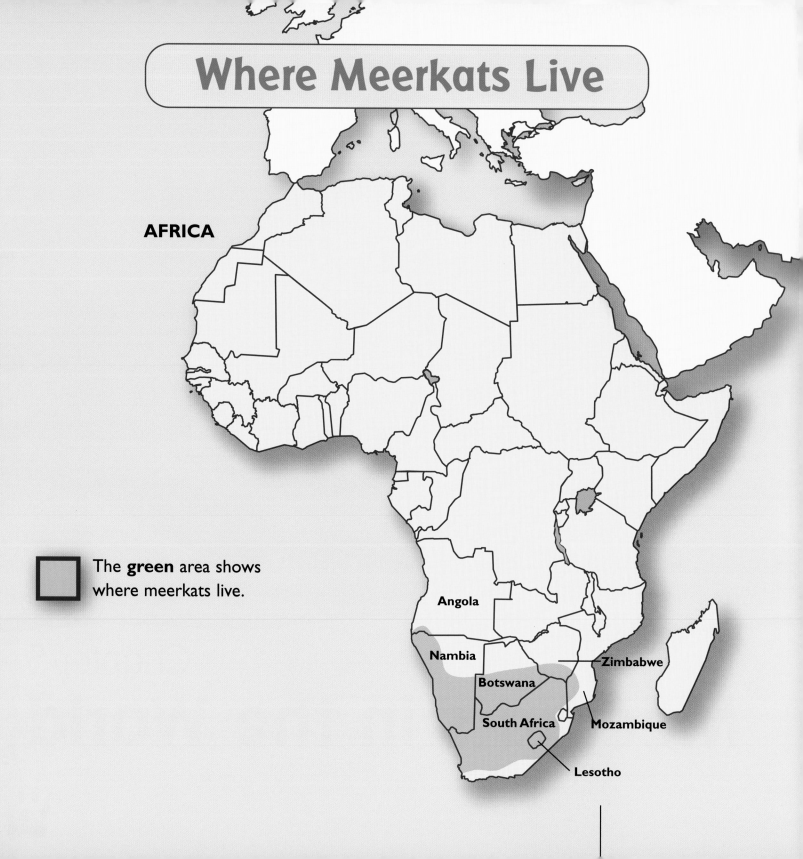

AFRICA

The **green** area shows where meerkats live.

Angola

Nambia

Botswana

Zimbabwe

South Africa

Mozambique

Lesotho

Where Meerkats Live

Meerkats live in and around the Kalahari Desert in southern Africa. Their homes can be found in the countries of Angola, Namibia, Botswana, Zimbabwe, Mozambique, Lesotho, and South Africa.

Meerkat country is hot and dry. Each year usually brings some big rainstorms. But there are times when it doesn't rain for many months. These periods are called droughts (pronounced *DROWTS*). During a long drought, desert plants can shrivel and die, and the insects and other animals that depend on them for food can die too. The meerkats then need to move farther and farther away from their usual territory to find food. If all of the mob members are hungry and busy looking for food, then there are fewer members able to act as guards. This leaves the weakest meerkats as easy prey for attackers.

Africa's Angels

In some parts of Africa, the meerkat is known as the sun angel because it loves the sun so much. Some people used to believe that sun angels protected their villages from moon devils. Moon devils is another term for werewolves, imaginary men that became wolflike creatures and attacked stray cattle—and even people.

The Future of Meerkats

Meerkats exist in large numbers and are not considered to be endangered. Perhaps that is because humans are not particularly interested in moving into their territories.

However, the life of a meerkat is not an easy one. Natural threats are droughts, burrow-flooding rainstorms, and attacks by predators. Kits are the most affected by these events. In fact, only one kit in four survives its first year.

Smaller mobs have more trouble surviving than larger mobs. Fewer meerkats means less help with kits and fewer guards to take turns watching for predators. Colonies of fifteen to thirty seem to have the best chance of survival.

Fast Facts About Meerkats

Scientific name	*Suricata suricatta*
Class	Mammalia
Order	Carnivora
Size	Up to 20 inches from head to tip of tail
Weight	Up to 2 pounds
Life span	Up to 14 years
Habitat	Burrows in dry, desertlike lands

Meerkats have learned that they need to stay together to survive.

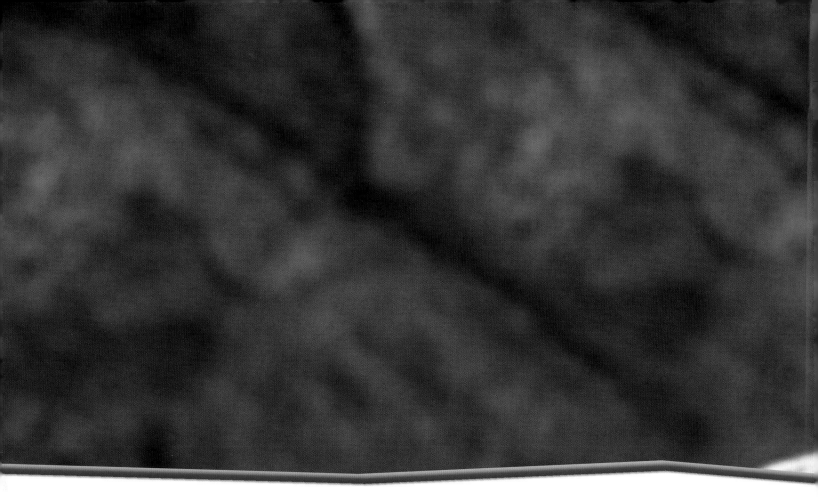

Glossary of Wild Words

alpha female   lead female of the mob. She is usually the only one to give birth.

alpha male   lead male of a mob. He is usually the only one to mate with the alpha female.

balance   the ability to stay steady

carnivore   a meat-eating animal

communication   the exchange of thoughts, feelings, and information through signs and sounds

habitat   the natural environment where an animal or plant lives

kit   a baby meerkat

mammal	an animal with a backbone and hair on its body that drinks milk from its mother when it is born	**regulate**	to control
		species	a group of plants or animals that are the same in many ways
mob	a group of meerkats. This group is also called a colony.	**territory**	an area of land that an animal considers to be its own and will fight to defend
poisonous	containing a harmful or deadly poison		
predators	animals that hunt and eat other animals to survive	**venom**	poisonous fluid that some animals introduce into the bodies of prey by biting or stinging
prey	animals that are hunted by other animals for food		

Index